How to Art Doodle™

Printing

& Other Amazing Techniques

Carolyn Scrace

This edition first published in MMXV by
Book House

Distributed by Black Rabbit Books
P.O. Box 3263
Mankato
Minnesota MN 56002

Cataloging-in-Publication Data is available
from the Library of Congress

HB ISBN: 978-1-909645-51-6
PB ISBN: 978-1-910184-38-7

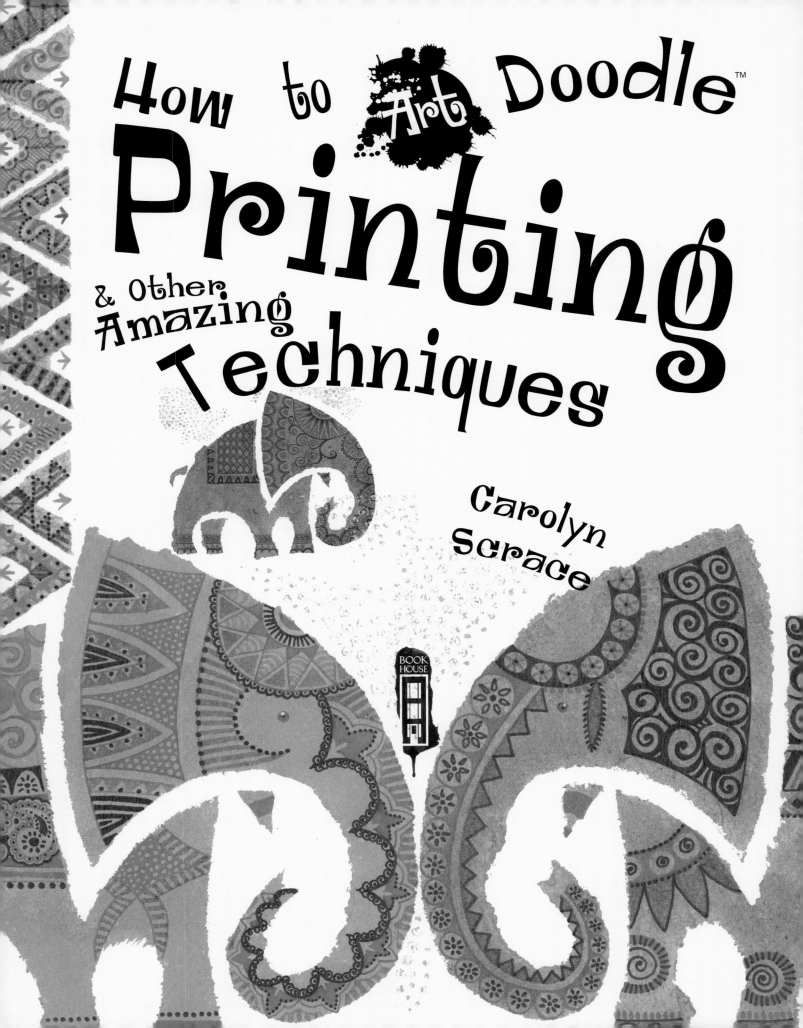

How to Art Doodle™

Printing

& Other Amazing Techniques

Carolyn Scrace

BOOK HOUSE

Contents

Please note: Sharp blades and scissors should be used under adult supervision.

Introduction

This book explores some simple and effective printing techniques. It shows how to combine Art Doodling, printing, and other methods to produce visually stunning designs. Step-by-step guides lead you through from rough sketches to fabulous, finished artwork.

Art Doodling

Art Doodling releases creativity and develops drawing skills. Discover the added enjoyment of combining Art Doodle patterns with other artistic, fun techniques!

Inspiration

Inspiration is all around—before long you will start to see ideas for Art Doodle patterns and compositions everywhere—even in the most surprising places!

Sketchbook

Keep a small sketchbook or notepad with you at all times! Use it for experimental Art Doodling and to jot down ideas for future prints. Stick in any inspiring magazine cuttings and photographs you find, and remember to use the book as a work in progress!

Techniques

There are many different printing techniques. Most involve making a master printing block, the surface of which the artist draws on or into. The block is inked or painted, and paper is pressed onto it. The printed paper is peeled off and the process repeated to create more prints. The following three printing methods readily combine with Art Doodling.

Monoprinting

Monoprinting only produces one print from an image drawn or painted onto a smooth, flat surface like metal or glass. Paper is placed on top and pressed down. This transfers the image, in reverse.

Two monoprinting methods:

1. Paint an image directly onto glass or metal, lay paper on top, and press down to transfer the image.

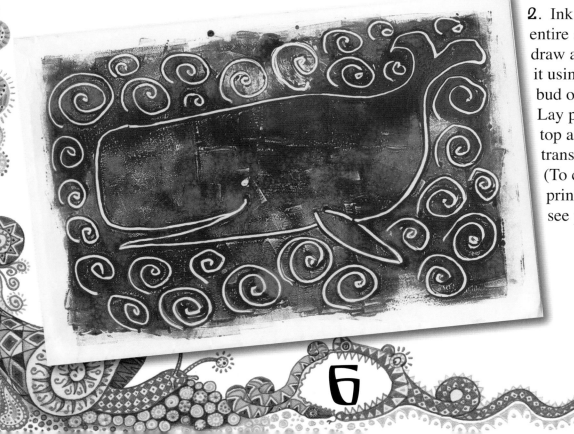

2. Ink or paint the entire surface then draw a picture into it using a cotton bud or finger tip. Lay paper on top and press to transfer the image. (To create this print of a whale, see page 14.)

Relief printing

A relief print is made when an artist cuts an image out of a flat surface like wood, linoleum, metal, or polystyrene. The printing block is created by the remaining "uncut" surface area. This is inked or painted, and then paper is pressed onto the wet surface. The image is transferred, in reverse, to the paper.

This relief print uses a polystyrene printing block (see pages 12–13).

Stenciling

A stencil is a sheet of paper (or other material) with designs cut out of it. Ink or paint is dabbed onto the cut out stencil to transfer the design onto any surface. The printed image will be an exact copy.

To stencil elephant shapes turn to pages 18–19.

Graphite pencils come in different grades, from hard to soft. Soft **pencil crayons** are ideal for adding color to indented designs.

Thick-tipped **marker pens** are perfect for filling in large areas. Fine-tipped, **permanent marker pens** are great for outlines and adding detail.

Pencil crayons

Tools & materials

A wide variety of equipment can be used for printmaking. This book describes how to use basic, readily available tools and materials. However, it is important to experiment—try to use whatever tools and materials inspire and excite you. Have fun discovering which pens produce the best Art Doodles on different print surfaces.

Wax crayons are ideal for creating scratch art or etched images.

Felt-tip pens come in a range of thicknesses.

Fineliner pens produce a flowing line. They work best when used over colored inks and watercolor paint.

A **black gel pen** is useful for outlines and detailed doodles. **Metallic and white gel pens** are ideal for doodling onto colored paper or over dark areas of color

Sponge

Scissors
(with blunt
ends)

String

Ruler

Ballpoint pen—a ballpoint pen that has run dry makes a good tool for indenting designs.

Polystyrene makes an ideal printing block. It can be purchased as sheets, or try using flat polystyrene food trays. Ideal for making printing blocks.

Sketchbook to jot down ideas and try out designs. Use your sketchbook for experimenting with new techniques. Keep notes about the materials and methods you used.

Types of paper

Cartridge paper comes in a variety of weights. Heavyweight paper is best for water-based paint. Note: ink lines may bleed (or run) on some cartridge papers.

Colored paper is ideal for printing different versions of the same image. It can be purchased as single sheets or in pads.

Clean **saucer** or dish for mixing paint.

Paintbrushes come in a wide range of shapes and sizes.

Gouache is opaque paint. Use for printing polystyrene blocks and for stenciling.

Brayer rollers come in a variety of widths. Choose one smaller than the print size. Use it to apply ink or paint to the surface of the printing block.

Poster paint is water soluble paint similar to gouache. It is great for experimenting. Use it for string printing, stenciling, and printing polystyrene blocks.

Block printing paint is ideal for printing techniques using a brayer roller.

string prints

In this relief printing technique, the raised printing surface is formed by a design made from string. A series of prints can be made from the same design.

You will need:
Cardboard
String
Washable glue
Scissors
Wide paintbrush
Poster paints
Colored paper
Black and white gel pens

1. Draw a design on your "printing block" (a piece of cardboard).

2. Now get messy! Cut a length of string, cover it with glue and position it on your design. Repeat.

3. Finish it off with a string border. Now seal the entire surface with a coat of glue. Leave until completely dry.

4. Paint the block with poster paint. Place paper on the wet surface, press down firmly then peel off.

5. Carefully wipe and dry the printing block before you change colors. Try printing onto darker shades of paper, and using contrasting colors. Leave the prints to dry.

6. Now Art Doodle some patterns following the lines of your design. Use white gel pen to doodle backgrounds on darker shades. Contrasting black and white doodles are useful for adding weight and impact.

Polystyrene prints

This form of relief printing uses polystyrene printing blocks. Design some wacky houses to print your own street scene or create an incredible city, as shown on the front cover!

1. Start by doing rough sketches of simple houses and trees.

2. Lightly trace or copy one house onto a piece of polystyrene. Now indent the lines using a "dry" ballpoint pen. Cut out the house shape.

3. Now paint your "house" printing block. Lay paper on top and use a wooden spoon to rub lightly over the surface. Carefully lift off the print. Leave to dry.

4. Art Doodle the house with black ball-point pen and fine felt tips. To print houses in different colors you will need to wipe and dry the printing block.

5. Print a row of houses, alternating the sizes, shapes, and colors to create an exciting composition.

6. Art Doodle the houses and add spiral-shaped plumes of smoke to some chimneys!

13

Monoprints

Monoprinting is a spontaneous technique. To make this print, ink is applied to a metal tray. Drawing on it removes some of the ink. This prints as a white line.

1. It is helpful to start with some thumbnail sketches of your design.

2. Cut the paper to fit the large tray. Load the roller with color then cover the large tray with paint. Draw your design on the wet surface using a cotton bud or your finger tip.

3. Lay the paper on top of the wet paint. Press down lightly using your hand. Gently peel the paper off to reveal the printed picture: the reversed image of a whale!

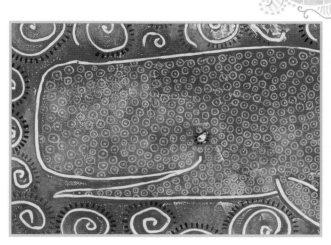

Ч. Use silver gel pen to Art Doodle the image. Dark colored felt-tip pens are ideal for doodling patterns around the swirls.

Ƨ. Frame your design using a sheet of colored paper larger than the print. Doodle the polystyrene fish pattern (see page 22).

Ƃ. Stick your whale print onto its "fishy" frame.

Wax etching

This design was inspired by the work of Pablo Picasso, a pioneer of cubism. Picasso combined two or more sides of his subject in the same painting to express three dimensions on a flat canvas.

You will need:
Wax crayons
Black gouache
Thick paintbrush
Empty ballpoint pen
Pencil for tracing

1. Make a detailed rough of your design. Plan which parts will be black and which will be in color.

2. Draw the curved outer border of your design on cartridge paper. Fill it in with a thick layer of pale-colored wax crayoning.

3. Paint over the wax-crayoning with dense, black gouache. Leave to dry. Lightly trace your design onto the black surface.

4. The areas to be kept black are outlined only by scratching into the paint with the empty ballpoint pen. Then start Art Doodling patterns to reveal the colored wax beneath.

Artist's tip: rest your drawing hand on
scrap paper to avoid marking the artwork.

stenciling

Print a series of stenciled elephants to create an exotic repeating pattern.

You will need:
Plastic project folder
Scissors or craft knife
White paper
Colored paper
Colored inks or
  poster paints
Sponge
Saucer
Ballpoint pen
Fineliner and gel pens
Gold gel pen

Warning: this project involves the use of a craft knife or scissors.

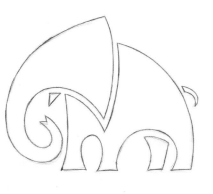

1. Draw an elephant. The simple shapes are separated by narrow gaps—see the ear, tusk, back leg, and tail.

2. Cut a piece of plastic to tape over the design. Trace the elephant using a ballpoint pen. Carefully cut out the template.

3. Place the template onto the paper. Using a sponge, gently dab color through the stencil cuts. Make four prints.

4. When the prints are dry, use fineliner pens to Art Doodle the elephants. Use similar colors but different patterns on each.

5. Design a stenciled border for your artwork. Print it on white paper for added contrast. Tear or cut out the border and stick in place. Art Doodle it using gel pens and the same color palette.

6. Use gold gel pen to Art Doodle simple patterns on the background.

Indenting

This simple technique produces delicate, white lines that are ideal for finely detailed Art Doodling. The end results can be both subtle and sophisticated.

You will need:
Thick cartridge paper
Empty ballpoint pen
Pencil crayons
Scrap paper
Black marker pen
Gold gel pen

1. Sketch a rough design to the size of the finished artwork. It is a good idea to plan your color scheme at this stage. Artist's tip: Use a limited palette and bold areas of color.

2. Lightly trace the outline of your design onto thick cartridge paper. Draw over the lines with "dry" ballpoint to indent. Start Art Doodling.

3. Lightly crayon over the indented lines. Do not press too hard. Rest your hand on scrap paper to prevent smudging.

4. Use black marker pen to fill in the background. This will make the main image stand out and add contrast to the design. Art Doodle over the background using a gold gel pen.

Pattern builder

These step-by-step examples show how to Art Doodle some of the patterns used in this book.

String prints (Pages 10-11)

1. Pencil curved outlines. Add a row of angled lines (as shown).

2. Pencil in opposing angled lines (as shown). Ink in all lines.

3. Use black ballpoint pen or grey fineliner shading to make the pattern look three-dimensional.

Monoprint (Pages 14-15)

1. Make a fish-shaped polystyrene printing block (see page 15). Print using gold gouache paint.

2. Once dry, outline the gold fish shapes using fine, black, felt-tip pen.

3. Art Doodle swirling water patterns using a fine black felt-tip and a gold gel pen.

Wax etching (Pages 16-17)

1. Gently pencil in guidelines. "Etch" in diagonals to make diamond shapes.

2. "Etch" a check pattern to alternate diamond shapes. Shade the check (as shown).

3. Leave the remaining diamond shapes black.

Glossary

Background   area behind an object or image.

Brayer   a roller used in printmaking to spread ink or paint.

Color palette   the range of colors used by an artist.

Color scheme   a planned combination of colors used in an artwork.

Composition   how an artist arranges shapes, sizes, and colors, the different elements that make a piece of art.

Cubism   style of art depicting several aspects of one object simultaneously.

Design   a graphic representation, usually a drawing or a sketch.

Etching   a printing process in which images are printed from metal plates.

Indenting   the process of making an image with an indented line.

Limited palette   when an artist restricts the number of colors used.

Linoleum   material used as floor covering.

Monoprint   a single print made by an artist painting or wiping a design directly onto a flat surface.

Polystyrene   smooth-surfaced foam plastic.

Printing block   surface from which an image can be printed.

Relief printing   printing from a raised surface.

Rough   a quick sketch of the main elements in a picture.

Sketch   a preparatory drawing.

Spontaneous   without thought or planning.

Stencil   a piece of paper, plastic card, or metal that has a design cut out of it.

Technique   an accepted method used to produce something.

Three-dimensional   having, or appearing to have, the dimension of depth, as well as width and height.

Thumbnail (sketches)   usually small, quick, abbreviated drawings.

Index